We Float Together

Remember Me

Roslyn Strohl

Illustrations Marcy Adams & Julie Frankel

Remember
dear one
to gather in your heart
the light
you knew to be me.

You can do this.
You will see.

You will find me
everywhere

scattered on
dew drops on
the grass

and on
the glinting crest
of waves.

I will twinkle
for you in the stars

and wink at night with the rabbit

in the round soft glow of the moon.

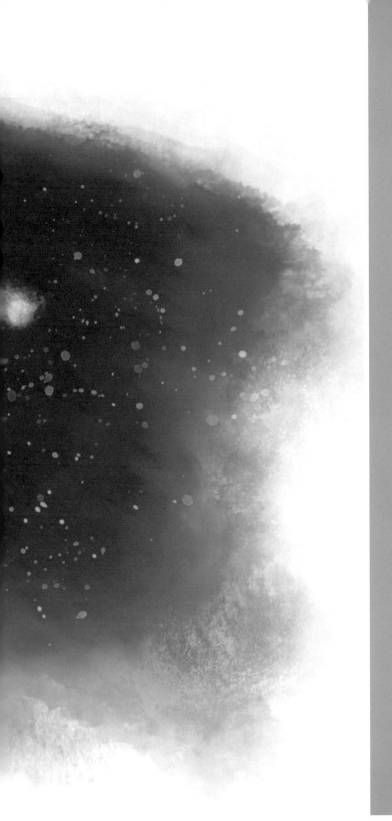

Look up to the sky,
the ink blue sky
my dear one.

Even when it is quiet
I am here,

The light in me
Finds the light
in you.

Feel how I **touch**
the palm of your hand
lightly

a tickle of kitten fur

the satin edge
of your blanket

a kiss
against your cheek.

Close
as your shadow
I will follow behind.

As long as you live
I am here.

This is how remembering works.
It is what we learn to do.

Remember
to remember me
As I remember you.

Through my rich life as teacher and therapist, children have guided me to the naturally wondrous and often wordless expression of the inner life. Children share in play how to unlock difficult experiences. Imagination and nature can knit the seams of past and present after loss. This book is written to us all in that spirit. It is meant to be read together and to open conversations.

I offer it in memory of my sister, Margaret Jann Southey, known as Maggie Jann to her dear grandchildren. I remember her laughter and how she loved the world.

Roslyn Strohl

Breathe,
Be Kind,
Choose Love

Remember Me

Remember dear one
to gather in your heart
the light
you knew to be me.
You can do this.
You will see.
You will find me everywhere
scattered on dew drops on the grass
and on the glinting crest of waves.
I will twinkle for you in the stars
and wink at night with the rabbit
in the round soft glow of the moon.

Look up to the sky, the ink blue sky
my dear one.
Even when it is quiet I am here,

The light in me
Finds the light in you.

Feel how I touch
the palm of your hand
lightly
a whisper of grass
a tickle of kitten fur
the satin edge
of your blanket
a kiss
against your cheek.

Close as your shadow
I will follow behind.
As long as you live
I am here.

This is how remembering works.
It is what we learn to do
Remember to remember me
As I remember you.

Remember Me

To order books contact: strohlroslyn@gmail.com

Copyright © 2023 by Roslyn Ann Strohl
All rights reserved. This book, or parts thereof, may not be reproduced in any form with out permission in writing from the author, Roslyn Ann Strohl.

Library of Congress Cataloging-in-Publication Data
1. Juvenile Fiction. 2. Family Relationships.
3. Death, Grief, Bereavement.
ISBN 979-8-9891036-0-7

ROSLYN ANN STROHL, Author

Raised and educated in Australia, Roslyn has taught in a variety of settings on three continents. In the early 80's, she refocused her work, embracing a variety of approaches to child and family systems therapy here in the U.S.

The past decade has been spent in Hospice counseling with individuals, families, and groups. With terminally ill, caregivers and those grieving she leaned into the attunement by which we offer each other healing.

A deep bow of acknowledgement to Hospice of San Luis Obispo County.

MARCY ADAMS & JULIE FRANKEL, Illustration and Design

Over the years we've enjoyed teaming up on illustration projects — blending our talents and skills. Our collaboration with Roslyn on this sensitive poem has been special. Marcy's personal goal of staying gender/ethnicity inclusive and age neutral was an interesting challenge and inspired us to emphasize access to the natural world as the connection to memories of our loved one.

Made in the USA
Columbia, SC
26 October 2023